FR. MARK TOUPS

Rejoice!

Finding Your Place in the Advent Story

DAILY MEDITATIONS FOR ADVENT

ASCENSION

West Chester, Pennsylvania

Nihil obstat: Rev. S Brice Higginbotham
               Censor Librorum
               August 24, 2021

Imprimatur: +Most Reverend Shelton J. Fabre
               Bishop of Houma-Thibodaux
               August 24, 2021

Unless otherwise noted, Scripture passages are from the *Revised Standard Version Bible*, Second Catholic Edition © 2006 by the Division of Christian Education of the National Council of the Churches of Christ in the United States of America. Used by permission. All rights reserved.

Scripture passages marked "NAB" are from the *New American Bible* © 1970, 1986, 1991, 2010 by the Confraternity of Christian Doctrine. All rights reserved.

Ascension
PO Box 1990
West Chester, PA 19380
1-800-376-0520
ascensionpress.com

Cover art: Mike Moyers (*Let Us Adore Him* © 2021 Mike Moyers, Franklin, TN)
Interior art: Mike Moyers (*Temple, Zechariah and Elizabeth, Caravan to Bethlehem, Preparation, Behold Him* © 2021 Mike Moyers, Franklin, TN)
Printed in the United States of America
ISBN 978-1-954881-00-6

CONTENTS

PREFACE

I started the *Rejoice!* series of Advent meditations because I longed to help people prepare for Christmas. As I prayed, I felt there was no better way to prepare for Christ's birth than with the two people who prepared for his birth during the very first Advent, namely, Mary and Joseph. As God inspired the writing, I grew to know Mary and Joseph personally. In *Rejoice! Advent Meditations with Mary,* I came to appreciate the humanity of the Blessed Mother, and, in *Rejoice! Advent Meditations with Joseph,* I came to appreciate the humanity of St. Joseph. As beautiful as those first two experiences were, I felt there was more to the story. I sensed God wanted to speak to the relationship between Mary and Joseph. This inspiration is what led me to write *Rejoice! Advent Meditations with the Holy Family.*

In previous *Rejoice!* meditations, I felt the Holy Spirit leading us to enter the hearts of Mary and Joseph, so in those Advent seasons, we focused on *their* hearts. As I carefully asked the Lord about this year's journey together, I felt his prompting for us all to focus on *our* hearts. So, this year, as we explore the world of the first Advent, the person we will come to know more is … *you.* This year, as we journey to Bethlehem, the meditations will help you enter your own heart.

The more I have prayed about that very first Advent, the more I have come to appreciate the *places*, *people*, and *events* that are a part of that story. And I have felt the Lord asking me to help us appreciate those important places, people, and events.

Each of us, especially at this time of year, is influenced by the places we live in, the people we know, and the events that are on our calendar. Think about that for just a moment. Consider how much of your life is influenced by the places, people, and events of your everyday life. Perhaps few things influence us more.

As *Rejoice! Finding Your Place in the Advent Story* follows the four weeks of Advent, it will help us appreciate the places, people, and events that complement the story of the very first Advent. In week one, we will explore several places in the Holy Land and what they teach us about the environment in which Mary and Joseph lived. In week two, we will come to appreciate several people who were preparing for the birth of the Messiah while Mary and Joseph were preparing for the birth of their son. In week three, we will look at the events that shaped the circumstances of Jesus' birth. In week four, we will enter into imaginative prayer to personally experience the final preparations for Christ's birth.

I pray that in deepening our appreciation of the places, people, and events of the very first Advent, we can encounter the Lord in our own lives and hearts during Advent this year. Enjoy Advent. Enjoy the journey. Enjoy the places, people, and events that shaped the story of the very first Advent and shape our own lives now.

GETTING THE MOST OUT OF *REJOICE!*

The journal that you have in your hands is an Advent prayer journal with daily meditations by Fr. Mark Toups and with artwork by Mike Moyers. It is the fourth in an ongoing series of *Rejoice!* journals. The others are *Advent Meditations with Mary, Advent Meditations with Joseph,* and *Advent Meditations with the Holy Family.* Each journal is designed to be used by parishes, small groups, and individuals in preparation for Christmas.

Community

Community is a key component of the journey to holiness. Advent provides a wonderful opportunity to take a little more time to focus on your prayer life and grow stronger in friendships on the shared journey to heaven.

The ideal is for a whole parish to take up *Rejoice!* and journey together as a community. You can learn more about how to provide *Rejoice!* to a large parish group at **rejoiceprogram.com**. There is also information about bulk discounts and parish mission nights with the *Rejoice!* videos. If you are not able to experience *Rejoice!* as a whole parish, consider a small group setting. Use *Rejoice!* as a family devotion for Advent, or get together with a few friends to discuss how God is speaking to you in this season. Bulk pricing for small groups is available. You might also want to use *Rejoice!* as an individual. You can take this journey through Advent even if you are not meeting in a group or talking about it with friends. You are not alone—Catholics all over the country are on the same journey. This journal is a place for you to speak to God and to hear and see all that he has to show you.

Videos

To accompany the journal, *Rejoice!* offers videos with Fr. Mark Toups, Sr. Miriam James Heidland, and Fr. Josh Johnson. Through their witness, conversation, and prayer, you will find fresh insights into the places, people, and events of the first Advent.

The program includes a primary *Rejoice!* video and weekly themed videos. Each Sunday of Advent, you will get access to a quick video to energize your reflections and encourage you in your prayer that week. Sign up for these weekly videos at **rejoiceprogram.com** to receive them by email.

Daily Meditation and Prayer

Each week's meditations and videos take you into the places and introduce you to the people and events leading up to Jesus' birth. Each day, a new meditation invites you to consider prayerfully the world you live in now in the light of the first Advent. It prompts you to prepare your heart, not just for Christmas Day but for the birth of Christ.

The day's reflection ends with a prompt titled "For Your Prayer." During the first three weeks of Advent, this section gives you a Scripture passage to read and a prompt to help you bring your heart to the Lord in prayer. In the fourth week, the meditations will feel different as they shift to guided, imaginative prayer. These meditations set a scene based in Scripture, and "For Your Prayer" invites you to enter that scene as you pray. You will recognize some of the places, people, and events from earlier meditations, but you will encounter them now in a new way.

Since the fourth week of Advent varies in length from year to year, we have provided seven meditations for that week. So, whether the fourth week this Advent is two days or seven days long, you will have enough content for each day of the season.

Here is how to pray with both the Scripture passages and the Scripture-based scenes.

Prepare

If you are praying with Scripture, open your Bible and read the passage once. If you are praying imaginatively, read through the scene. Get familiar with the words. Then slowly read the text a second time.

Pay attention to how you feel as you read. Pay attention to which words strike you. When the text sets a scene, enter the scene with Mary and Joseph or the other people mentioned. Once the passage or the scene comes to its natural conclusion, continue with ARRR.

ARRR

ARRR stands for **A**cknowledge, **R**elate, **R**eceive, and **R**espond. You have sat with God's Word. You have entered into the scene. Now, when you feel that God is saying something to you, *acknowledge* what stirs within you. Pay attention to your thoughts, feelings, and desires. These are important. After you have acknowledged what is going on inside your heart, *relate* that to God. Don't just think about your thoughts, feelings, and desires. Don't just think about God or how God might react. Relate to God. Tell him how you feel. Tell him what you think. Tell him what you want. Share all your thoughts, feelings, and desires with God. Share everything with him. Once you have shared everything with God, *receive*. Listen to what he is telling you. It could be a subtle voice you hear. It could be a memory that pops up. Maybe he invites you to reread the Scripture passage. Perhaps he invites you into a still, restful silence. Trust that God is listening to you, and receive what he wants to share with you.

Now *respond*. Your response could be continuing your conversation with God. It could be resolving to do something. It could be tears or laughter. Respond to what you are receiving.

Journal

The last step is to *journal*. Keep a record this Advent of what your prayer was like. Your journal entry does not have to be lengthy. It could be a single word or a sentence or two about what God told you or how the day's reflection struck you. However you do it, journaling will help you walk closer to God this Advent. We have provided space for you in this journal each day.

Commit

Advent can be a busy season. As you dedicate yourself to prayer this Advent, there is no better safeguard than a good plan. Fr. Josh Johnson, one of the presenters in the *Rejoice!* videos, recommends the five Ws as a method of planning. Here is how it works. Every Sunday, look at your calendar and write out your plan for the next six days, answering the following questions: When? Where? What? Who? and Why?

WHEN will I spend time with Jesus?

WHERE will I spend time with Jesus?

WHAT are Jesus and I going to do together?

WHO will hold me accountable for my time with Jesus?

WHY am I prioritizing my time with Jesus?

Making a commitment is the first step in transforming your prayer life. These weeks with *Rejoice! Finding Your Place in the Advent Story* are the perfect time to begin.

The First Week of Advent

Places

"Faithfulness will spring
up from the ground,
and righteousness
will look down from
heaven. … [T]he Lord
will give what is good."

—Psalm 85:11-12

WHERE WE ARE

influences who we are. Where we are influences how we think, feel, and act. It shapes our values and priorities and is the lens through which we see the world. The places that Mary and Joseph knew also reveal much about God. If we truly want to come to appreciate what God is doing in the Advent story, then we must come to appreciate what God is revealing about himself in the places of ancient Israel.

The places that shaped the very first Advent did so by influencing Mary and Joseph. Some of these places, such as Nazareth and Bethlehem, are explicitly mentioned in the Scriptures. Some of them, such as the Temple in Jerusalem and Herod's palace, are appreciated within a broader understanding of Israel's history.

Welcome to the first week of Advent. This week we shall learn more of how these places shaped the very first Advent.

SEARCHING

"Redeem Israel,

O God, out of

all his troubles."

—Psalm 25:22

What do I want from
God this advent

✱ Ps 37 - at the 3-7
heart of Jewish
spirituality

Trust; delight; be still

ISRAEL

If we are to appreciate the places of the very first Advent, it seems only right that we begin with Israel. The word Israel refers to both a nation and a land. At the birth of Christ, this land of "milk and honey" (Exodus 3:8) was a proud nation with a two-thousand-year history. A quick survey of its history can help us appreciate its influence on Mary and Joseph.

God formed a covenant with Abraham in approximately 2000 BC. Later, after the people had endured four hundred years of slavery in Egypt, Moses led Israel into freedom shortly before 1200 BC. From that time until 722 BC, God's Chosen People enjoyed extraordinary growth and blessing. Most of the Old Testament books were written during this time of blessing, including the book of Psalms, the Song of Songs, and the writings of many of the great prophets. Then, from 722 to 538 BC, Israel was a fallen nation. First, the northern kingdom was invaded by the Assyrians, and then the southern kingdom was exiled by the Babylonians. Yet, during this time of purification, there was still profound fruit, including the prophecies of Isaiah and Jeremiah.

During the first fifteen hundred years of Israel's history, there was extraordinary evidence of God's Providence. However, the five hundred years immediately preceding Christ's birth were different. When the Jews returned from exile in Babylon, their great Temple was in ruins. Then, in 322 BC, just when they were back on their feet, they were conquered by the Greeks and occupied by them for more than one hundred and fifty years. Then, less than one hundred years after they reclaimed their freedom from the Greeks, the Romans conquered them and took control in 63 BC.

ache - longed for something

In short, the five hundred years preceding the birth of Christ challenged Israel's very identity. First the Greeks and then the Romans occupied its lands. There were no more prophets, no more great leaders, and no glorious victories of which to boast. At the time of the very first Advent, Israel was searching for identity, direction, and evidence of God's provision. The interior searching of the nation would have echoed in the hearts of Mary and Joseph. Many of us may identify with this searching, as many of us may also be searching. Perhaps you are searching for identity, direction, and evidence of God's provision. Perhaps you are searching for peace in your heart or in your vocation or your family. Perhaps you are searching for freedom, healing, or forgiveness. Maybe there was a time in your life when God felt real, but lately he seems absent. Perhaps you are searching for God, and you do not yet know what that might look like. As we begin this journey of Advent, ask yourself where you are with God. This Christmas, what do you want from God? What do you really want? What are you searching for?

For your prayer

Begin by reading Psalm 25. Consider how often Mary and Joseph would have prayed with the very same words you are reading. Read it a few times. What is God saying to you in the Bible passage? How does it apply to your life? What do you want to say to God? What are you searching for?

"Father, I beg you to make this Advent my best ever. Help me to find you deep within. Reveal to me what it is I am really searching for."

Ps 25

What words stood out to you as you prayed?
What did you find stirring in your heart?

V. 2 (In You I trust; (me) let
me not be put to
shame — (Patrick whose
day in court is tomorrow
11/23/21)

V. 3 (let not my enemies exaut
over me — no one who
→ waits for You shall be
put to shame

V. 5 Me — Teach me Your ways,
guide me on Your paths

V. 7 Patrick — The sins of my
youth + my frailties
remember not

V. 11 For Your namesake You
will pardon my guilt

WANT

"You have given him
his heart's desire."

—Psalm 21:2

TEMPLE

To understand the places that shaped the hearts of Mary and Joseph, one must appreciate the significance of the Temple in Jerusalem. Let us start at the beginning. The first commandment is first for a reason: "I am the LORD your God, who brought you out of the land of Egypt, out of the house of bondage. You shall have no other gods before me" (Exodus 20:2-3). God's first commandment is for us to worship him *and him alone*. The worship of God is so important to God that he himself determines *how* we worship and eventually *where* we worship. In the Old Testament, the offering of sacrifice was not merely central to the worship of God; there was no worship of God without sacrifice. Remember, for example, the blood of the lambs on the lintels and doorposts on the first Passover in Exodus 12. That night, before they fled Egypt, the people worshipped God by offering him sacrifice, and they applied the blood of the sacrifice to the lintels and doorposts of their homes. That blood was not merely an indication of *where* the Israelites were; it was an indication of *whose* the Israelites were. The blood on the lintels and doorposts was the blood of the sacrificed Passover lamb. It showed that the people belonged to the one true God.

In 957 BC, the Temple that King Solomon built in Jerusalem was completed, and it quickly became the place for all Israelites to offer sacrifice. In fact, Exodus 23:14-17 explicitly outlines how all adult men in Israel were to go on pilgrimage to the Temple in Jerusalem three times a year. By the seventh century BC, the Temple was *the* center of the world for the Israelites, for it was *the* place to offer sacrifice. Solomon's Temple was destroyed in 586 BC at the hands of the Babylonians. The southern kingdom was taken captive, and so began the Babylonian exile. In 538 BC, as exiled Jews began to return to Jerusalem, they started to rebuild the Temple, and, by 515 BC, this second Temple was completed. But the new Temple was not as splendid as Solomon's original one. At the time of Mary and Joseph, there were many in Israel who longed for the Temple to be restored to its original glory. Appreciative of what they had, many wanted more. There is grace in *why* they wanted more, and it is important for us to recognize *that they wanted* more.

God created us to want, to desire. What we want, what we *really* want, indicates where God is and what God is doing in our lives. To further assist you in the naming of your desires, return to yesterday's reflection and ask yourself what you are searching for. If we are going to receive what we want, we have to be specific. The more specific we are in naming our desires, the more disposed we are to receive the very things we want. Most of us remain unsatisfied because we fail to specifically name what we want. So ask yourself again: What do you want from God? What do you *really* want?

For your prayer

Begin by reading Psalm 21. Read it a few times. Consider how often Mary and Joseph would have prayed with the very same words you are reading. What do you *really* want from God? Allow yourself to ask this question in earnest, and open yourself to the answer.

"Father, help me to be present to the present moment. Reveal to me what you want for me and what my deepest desires are."

What words stood out to you as you prayed?
What did you find stirring in your heart?

The long + me today have eternal life " endless days "

You grant our heart's desire —

let me want what you want

PROFOUND

" ... after the fire
a still small voice.
And ... Elijah
heard it. "

—1 Kings 19:12-13

GALILEE

Galilee is a region of northern Israel with the Mediterranean Sea on its western border and the Sea of Galilee on its eastern border. The mountains of northern Galilee are rugged terrain, but its southern border is a land of rolling hills and fertile plains. By the beginning of the first century, Galilee was already considered a place of little worth. It was far from Jerusalem, of course. But it had also been known for generations for the twenty towns that King Solomon gave to King Hiram, a foreigner, in payment for his help in building the Temple—towns that even back then "did not please" the foreign king (1 Kings 9:12). Now, many foreigners lived there, and the region was regarded with contempt. In short, the region of Galilee was insignificant.

The simple hiddenness of Galilee would have shaped the humility and receptivity of Mary and Joseph. Both were at peace with the ordinary, and the simplicity of life in Galilee would have nurtured their capacity to find God with them in ordinary days. For us, Advent is preceded by the *extra*ordinary intensity of Thanksgiving, Black Friday, Cyber Monday, and Giving Tuesday. And Advent is followed immediately by the extraordinary celebration of Christmas, with its presents and holiday banquets. In between are the decorations and music that fill our houses, our streets, and our grocery stores. In our Advent, we are steeped in the extraordinary.

Perhaps the insignificance of Galilee can teach us much at this time of year. Let me explain. Fr. George Aschenbrenner, SJ, once said that we should not confuse intensity with profundity. Just because an experience is intense does not mean it is profound. Much of the extraordinary around us is merely intense. Sometimes the most profound moments are profound because they are real, for they touch the deepest realities of our real lives. Thus, many profound moments await us in the ordinary, for it is the ordinary where most of us live most of our lives.

Your ordinary is the Monday-to-Friday hum-drum of life. Your ordinary influences are your searching and wanting. If we are at peace in the ordinary, then we search less, for we are content. However, when we are unsettled or discontented, when our everyday lives do not satisfy us, we tend to fantasize about escape and hunt for diversion. No other time of the year gives us such an escape from the ordinary as the secular Christmas season, for we are only ever one shopping spree away from forgetting our discontent. The good news is that God lives *in the ordinary*. The profound is found in the ordinary. This Advent, be attentive to how God pursues you, but be aware that God's pursuit, and perhaps the most profound moments this Advent, will be found in the ordinary.

For your prayer

Begin by reading 1 Kings 19:9-12. Consider how often Mary and Joseph would have prayed with the very same words you are reading. Read it a few times. What is God saying to you in the Bible passage? How does it apply to your life? What do you want to say to God? Are you comfortable with the ordinary?

"Father, help me to be present to the present moment. Help me to find you in the ordinary of life."

What words stood out to you as you prayed?
What did you find stirring in your heart?

_____

_____

_____

_____

_____

_____

_____

_____

_____

_____

_____

_____

_____

_____

_____

_____

_____

_____

_____

_____

QUIET

Like a child that is
quieted is my soul.

—Psalm 131:2

NAZARETH

At the time of Mary's Annunciation, both she and Joseph lived in Nazareth, which had a population of less than five hundred. Nazareth was small, and its pace was slow, offering lots of silence and solitude. The quiet of Nazareth would have been matched by the prayerful quiet of Mary's and Joseph's hearts. We know that Mary and Joseph had contemplative spirits. For example, in Luke 2:19, we read that, shortly after the birth of Christ and the visit of the shepherds, "Mary kept all these things, pondering them in her heart." To ponder means to savor and consider in silence. In Matthew 1:19, we read that Joseph was "a just man," implying that Joseph was a man of profound holiness who was well versed in the Old Testament Scriptures. The description of Joseph as a "just man" also implies that Joseph was a man at home with silence and comfortable in solitude. Quiet was something that came easily in Nazareth. But when Mary and Joseph left Nazareth for Bethlehem, they would have had to be intentional to maintain their contemplative spirits amid the frenetic activity of the census.

Silence was an anchor for Mary and Joseph, for quiet was to their prayer as oxygen is to the body. The same is true for us. Simply put, we need quiet in order to be human. Finding time for quiet is difficult for many of us; however, at no other time of the year is it harder than it is now. Just as Mary and Joseph had to remain intentional for maintaining quiet amidst the news of the census, we, too, must be intentional if we are going to enjoy quiet as a regular part of our day. Quiet is not just going to happen. Therefore, there are three Ws that may help us remain intentional about creating space for silence. Ask yourself WHEN is the best time for you to be quiet? WHERE is the quietest place without interruptions? <u>WHO will hold you accountable</u> for remaining intentional about quiet?

To help with the quiet, let me make a recommendation: Reclaim control of your life. For one week, remove notifications on your phone. Adjust the settings on your phone to remove both the sounds and little red numbers. Then, put your phone on silent. <u>What you will discover is</u> this: Your <u>phone is the greatest source of noise in</u> your life. <u>Regain control</u> of your life by discovering just how <u>much</u> <u>we have become conditioned to yielding to our phones.</u> Try it for seven days, and discover how much noise you have eliminated.

Mary and Joseph's Advent journey led them to Bethlehem. This year's <u>Advent journey will lead you deep within</u> <u>yourself.</u> You will need time for quiet if <u>you are going to</u> <u>find what you</u> are searching for. Be not afraid. Be intentional about quiet.

For your prayer

Begin by reading Psalm 131. Consider how often Mary and Joseph would have prayed with the very same words you are reading. Read it a few times. <u>What is God saying to you in</u> <u>the Bible passage?</u> How does it apply to your life? What do you want to say to God? Are you comfortable with quiet?

"Father, help me to slow down, both externally and internally. Help me to quiet myself on both the outside and the inside."

↓ That I am not a proud
or boastful person +
That I do not spend

What words stood out to you as you prayed?
What did you find stirring in your heart?

time on complicated
matters that are
beyond me anyway.
I am content w/
my life mostly.

"My heart is not
proud"

That it ok to be
simple like M & J
were

PROMISE

" I know the plans I
have for you, says
the LORD … to
give you a future
and a hope. "

—Jeremiah 29:11

JUDEA

The region known as Judea is mentioned forty-four times in the New Testament and twenty-eight times in the Gospels alone. However, most of us do not know much about the place. Judea was a large region to the south of Galilee that included important cities such as Jerusalem and Bethlehem. Perhaps the most notable mention of Judea comes in Matthew 2:5-6, when the Magi respond to Herod's inquiries about where the Messiah was to be born. They respond by quoting the prophet Micah: "In Bethlehem of Judea; for so it is written by the prophet: 'And you, O Bethlehem, in the land of Judah, are by no means least among the rulers of Judah; for from you shall come a ruler who will govern my people Israel.'" Judea is an important place in the Advent story, for God made a promise that the Messiah would be born "in the land of Judah" (Matthew 2:6).

God's people were familiar with his promises. God made a promise to Abraham that his descendants would be as numerous as the stars in the sky and would inhabit the land promised to them. God promised Moses that he would free his people from the slavery of Egypt and lead them to this promised land. Though they were later exiled and enslaved again by the Babylonians, God again promised his people through Isaiah and Jeremiah that he would free them again and lead them back to their own land. God is a God of promises, and, to those awaiting the birth of the Messiah at the time of the first Advent, Judea would have been a place that reminded them of those promises. While God used Jeremiah to promise Israel they would return home from their exile, God also made another promise to Israel that would sustain them during their exile: "Then you will call upon me and come and pray to me, and I will hear you. You will seek me and find me; when you seek me with all your heart, I will be found by you, says the LORD" (Jeremiah 29:12-14).

God wants to be found. He wants to be heard and known. However, this time of year can present particular challenges to hearing and knowing him. For some of us, it is the challenge of calendar, pace, and lack of quiet. For others, it may be dealing with the expectations, circumstances, and emotions that we find in our hearts if we do get quiet. The reason that so many of us are uncomfortable with silence is because we are not convinced that God is there in the silence. Be encouraged, for he *is* there. He *promised.*

Be not afraid this Advent. God wants to be with you. He wants to be found. He promised.

For your prayer

Begin by reading Jeremiah 29:11-14. Consider how often Mary and Joseph would have prayed with the very same words you are reading. Read it a few times. What is God saying to you in the Bible passage? How does it apply to your life? What do you want to say to God? What is his promise saying to you?

"Father, help me to be not afraid of silence. Help me to find you with me, deep within, in the silence."

What words stood out to you as you prayed?
What did you find stirring in your heart?

UNFULFILLED

> "My word … shall accomplish that which I intend."
>
> **—Isaiah 55:11**

PALACE

Yesterday, we learned how Judea was a place that reminded the Jews of God's promises. However, deep in the heart of that region was Jerusalem, and the king's palace in Jerusalem was a place that mocked other promises. When God chose Israel as his own, he originally intended for them to be governed by the priesthood. However, eventually Israel noticed that other kingdoms were ruled by kings, and they soon asked God for a king (see 1 Samuel 8). God relented and gave Israel their kings, the greatest of whom was King David. We read of God's promise to David: "When your days are fulfilled and you lie down with your fathers, I will raise up your offspring after you, who shall come forth from your body, and I will establish his kingdom. He shall build a house for my name, and I will establish the throne of his kingdom for ever. I will be his father, and he shall be my son" (2 Samuel 7:12-14).

What did this mean? God promised that the Messiah would come from David's line. However, as part of that promise, God promised David that his offspring would lead the kingdom of Israel. Two thousand years ago, this promise seemed to be unfulfilled. Judea was occupied by the Romans, and the Romans had appointed their own king, the hated King Herod, as their puppet. Herod's rule as "king" would have been a mockery to the Jews. Not only was Herod not of David's lineage; Herod was not even Jewish. Herod's father was by descent an Edomite, whose ancestors had converted to Judaism.

The greatest city in Judea was Jerusalem, and Herod's palace was in the center of the upper city. His palace towered over Jerusalem as a place that would have pierced the hearts of the people of Israel. It mocked God's promises and tempted the Jews to think that God's promise of the Messiah might never be fulfilled. Sometimes you and I also find ourselves in circumstances that make us doubt whether God will come through on his promises. Unanswered prayers, especially those we begged God for during times of suffering, can erode our trust in him and tempt us to doubt his promises. In addition, no other time of the year has expectations higher than they are now, in Advent. Unmet expectations, especially the expectations of the people or circumstances most personal to us, can also weaken our trust in God's promises. Look deep within. How are you doing with God's promises?

For your prayer

Begin by reading Isaiah 55:10-13. Consider how often Mary and Joseph would have prayed with the very same words you are reading. Read it a few times. What is God saying to you in the Bible passage? Specifically, what is God saying to you about his promises?

"Father, reveal to me how I may have been affected by unmet expectations or unfulfilled promises. Reveal to me how this has affected our relationship."

What words stood out to you as you prayed?
What did you find stirring in your heart?

_____
_____
_____
_____
_____
_____
_____
_____
_____
_____
_____
_____
_____
_____
_____
_____
_____
_____
_____
_____

FULFILLED

"Take delight in the LORD, and he will give you the desires of your heart."

—Psalm 37:4

BETHLEHEM

There can be no mention of the places of Advent without mention of Bethlehem. After all, it is to Bethlehem that the season of Advent is leading us. Bethlehem is the place where the promise *was to be* fulfilled, and Bethlehem is indeed where that promise *was* fulfilled. Why Bethlehem? Yesterday, we learned of the promise that God made in 2 Samuel. David was born in Bethlehem, and, thus, the "City of David" was Bethlehem. Furthermore, Micah's prophecy clearly stated that the Messiah would be born in Bethlehem. Interestingly, the Hebrew word *beth* means "house," and *lehem* means "bread." *Bethlehem* literally translates as the "house of bread," a fascinating foreshadowing of the One who was to be born in Bethlehem, who is the "Bread of Life." Bethlehem is not just *a* place. It is *the* place where the promise was fulfilled.

Let us pause for a moment and revisit the key words and movements of this First Week of Advent. We are all *searching* for something in life. Most of us want to be happy, but for sure no other time of year reveals the fact that we all *want* something. The question, of course, is what do you want? More importantly this Advent, what are you *searching* for? We often search in the externals of life, hoping that in the "things" of this world we will find what we are searching for. But wisdom tells us that it is in the *quiet* that we discover the more *profound* things of life. What often prevents us from looking deep within is the ache of *unfulfilled* expectations, or unfulfilled *promises*. We cannot see, touch, or feel our interior life as easily as we can our physical, sensual world. Moreover, our hearts often contain things that many of us would rather not look at. In fact, the secular Christmas season often reminds us of who is not there, what did not happen, and how we did not get this or that.

There are three things that are interesting about Bethlehem. First, Mary and Joseph would have never gone to Bethlehem unless they had to. They were led to go to Bethlehem. Second, the journey to Bethlehem would have been more difficult than they expected. For example, both Mary's pregnancy and Joseph's poverty would have presented challenges that we often do not think about. Third, their arrival in Bethlehem did not unfold the way that they expected. Because there was no room for them in the inn, Jesus was actually born on the outskirts of the city. Our interior journeys this Advent may be a lot like Mary and Joseph's journey to Bethlehem. For many of us, the only way we will go deep is if we are led. That journey may be more difficult than you expect, and it may not unfold the way you expect. However, I promise you this: God is with you. The same God who fulfilled the promise in Bethlehem is the same God who is with you now.

For your prayer

Begin by reading Psalm 37:1-7. Look back on the first week of Advent. What were the themes? What did God say? As the First Week concludes, ask again, what do you *really* want from God?

"Father, help me to trust you. Help me to follow you. Give me the grace I need to follow you wherever you desire to lead me this Advent."

What words stood out to you as you prayed?
What did you find stirring in your heart?

_____

_____

_____

_____

_____

_____

_____

_____

_____

_____

_____

_____

_____

_____

_____

_____

_____

_____

_____

The Second Week of Advent

People

"I will leave in the midst of you a people humble and lowly. They shall seek refuge in the name of the LORD."

—**Zephaniah 3:12-13**

WHEN WE THINK

of Advent, we often think of Mary and Joseph, and rightly so, for they are the central characters in the Advent narrative. However, we know that there were others waiting for the Messiah. The Gospels tell us about some of these people by name: Zechariah and Elizabeth, Simeon, and Anna. We can also imagine that Mary's own parents were awaiting the birth of their grandson. These people each waited for the Messiah in their own way, and each of them has something to teach us.

Welcome to the second week of Advent. This week we shall learn more how these people were waiting during the very first Advent.

OFFER

"All your works

shall give thanks

to you, O LORD."

—**Psalm 145:10**

JOACHIM AND ANNE

There is no mention of Mary's parents in the Bible. What we know of Joachim and Anne comes from the living tradition of the Church. However, there is an important detail of Mary's life that tells us much about her parents. Every year, on November 21, we celebrate the liturgical memorial of the Presentation of Mary. Roots of this date back to liturgical texts of the eighth century. Tradition tells us that when Mary was three years old, her parents, Joachim and Anne, took her to the Temple in Jerusalem to consecrate her for special service to the Lord. According to tradition, it is likely that Mary grew up in the Temple and remained there until she was twelve years old, when she would have returned home to Nazareth. Mary's parents offered her to the Lord. One can infer that while they took her to the Temple when she was three years old, they may have offered her to God in their hearts long before that, perhaps even before she was born. Despite what we do not know about her parents, what we do know is that they had hearts that offered to God what was most sacred to them.

This time of year can lure us into a self-focused posture of receiving. In other words, even as we buy gifts for others, we can easily become preoccupied with the presents we will be getting *from* others. Furthermore, unless we become intentional about our spiritual reformation, many of us are conditioned into a pattern where our prayer focuses on what we need from God or what we need God to do in our lives.

What can we learn from Joachim and Anne? When we willingly offer God what is most sacred to us, we create space in our hearts to receive more from him, who "is able to do far more abundantly than all that we ask or think" (Ephesians 3:20).

For example, let us start with worry. Many of us may pray about the things that we are worried about. Many of us may want God to do something in a particular situation, and we think that, if he does, our worries will go away. We are focused on a particular outcome. But we grow spiritually when, instead, we offer the outcome to God. In surrendering the outcome rather than clinging in prayer to a particular fix, we give God complete freedom to do what is best for us. If we are anchored in the reality that God does indeed want only what is best for us, we offer him the outcome, asking only that he act in the way that is best for us, for another person, or for the situation.

Joachim and Anne teach us how to offer what we cherish. This Advent, can you offer God your vocation, your family, and your finances? Can you offer the outcomes you most hope for? Can you offer God the outcomes connected to the people, situations, and problems that worry you most?

For your prayer

Begin by reading Psalm 145. Consider how often Joachim and Anne, as well as Mary and Joseph, would have prayed with the very same words you are reading. Read the Psalm a few times. What is God saying to you in this Bible passage?

"Father, help me to trust you. Give me the grace to let you answer my prayers when and how it is best for me."

What words stood out to you as you prayed?

What did you find stirring in your heart?

Do I believe God has the best in mind for me?

Do I ache? What is my pain?

Where do I need Jesus to touch & heal?

Ps 145
The Lord is kind & merciful; slow to anger & abounding in kindness

DOUBT

"Hope in God. … I shall
again praise him."

—Psalm 43:5

ZECHARIAH

The Advent story in Luke 1 speaks much of Zechariah. So who was Zechariah, and what can we learn from him? Zechariah was the husband of Elizabeth, the father of John the Baptist, and a priest of the division of Abijah. The Bible tells us that when Zechariah and his wife, Elizabeth, were old and without children, Zechariah was visited by the archangel Gabriel and told that they would have a son. But Zechariah doubted the angel's promise. In response, he was rendered unable to speak until the birth of his son (see Luke 1:5-20). Fortunately, as the story unfolds, God restored Zechariah's voice after he confirmed John's name at the baby's circumcision.

There are two distinct messages from an angel in Luke 1: the message to Zechariah about the conceiving of John and the message to Mary about the conceiving of Jesus. Notice that Zechariah and Mary both express doubt when they hear the angel's message. But Mary wonders *how* God will work the miracle (see Luke 1:34). Zechariah, however, doubts that God *can* work the miracle (see Luke 1:18). Mary questions how she, a virgin, can conceive a child. Zechariah doubts God's power and providence, a doubt most likely rooted in the grief and disappointment of many years of unanswered prayers for children. Zechariah's doubt could have stemmed from unmet expectations, a projection onto God of the pain and grief in his heart.

Mike

What can we learn from Zechariah? It is important to understand the influence of unanswered prayers or unmet expectations. Yesterday, I encouraged you to offer God the most sacred things of your life. I did so assuming that we are anchored in the reality that God indeed wants only what is best for us. That is a great question for you to behold: Do you believe—*are you absolutely convinced*—that God wants only what is best for you? We have read about God's miracles in the Bible, and we have learned about God's miracles since then. We hear about God's miracles in other people's lives. But for many of us reading this, the reason we cling to the materialism of "the world" or keep grasping for control of our lives is because, while we do not like to admit it, we really do not believe that God wants only what is best for us. Why do *we* doubt? Why would we doubt that God wants only what is best for us? Just as Zechariah's doubt may have stemmed from unmet expectations, a projection onto God of the pain and grief in his heart, so, too, do many of us have unanswered prayers that have left us doubting. Learning from yesterday's offering of outcomes, many of us have begged God for miracles, and we often assume that our prayer was not answered because a specific outcome did not come to fruition. The more unanswered prayers we face, the easier it is to doubt, especially when we thought that those specific outcomes would make us happy. Stay with me. Trust the process. Today's prayer will be important.

For your prayer

Begin by reading Psalm 43. Consider how often Zechariah would have prayed with the very same words you are reading. Now, ask yourself: Do *you* believe—*are you absolutely convinced*—that God wants only what is best for you?

"Father, help me to trust you. Reveal to me if there is any doubt in my heart, and be with me there so that I might know your fidelity."

What words stood out to you as you prayed?
What did you find stirring in your heart?

Ps 43 V 2
For you oh God
are my strength
V 3
send forth your
light & fidelity
they shall God
me on & bring
me to your holy
mountain
V 5
I hope in God

PROVIDE

" Give thanks
to the Lord …
who alone does
great wonders. "

—Psalm 136:3-4

JOHN THE BAPTIST

Let us stay with yesterday's prayer. Do you believe that God wants only what is best for you? As we look to the end of the story of Zechariah, we learn something more: What God provides for us is infinitely better than what we can provide for ourselves. For years, Zechariah asked for *a* child. In the end, God provided a child, but not just *any* child. God provided Zechariah a child who was John the Baptist. Jesus would later say of John the Baptist that "among those born of women none is greater than John" (Luke 7:28). So, while Zechariah wanted a child, God wanted the *best* for Zechariah. God did not want merely the good; God wanted *the best* for him. Thus, God blessed Zechariah with the best child Zechariah could imagine, for what God provides for us is infinitely better than what we can provide for ourselves. The journey of this particular Advent hinges on these two realities: that God wants only what is best for us and that what God can provide for us is infinitely better than what we can provide for ourselves. This is a game-changer, if we believe it. It is life-changing, if we let ourselves be guided and governed by it.

Think about how much energy we expend either because we do not really believe God wants only what is best for us or because we do not really believe that what God will provide for us is better than what we can provide for ourselves. Really. May I ask you to put down this book now? Stop for a moment and consider how much of your life you are living outside of those two realities. There is good news for you this Advent. God is *real*. In a world seduced by modern-day atheism, I repeat to you: God is *real*. This Advent, we are not merely preparing for a baby. We are preparing to receive the reality that God is *real*. God has a face.

He has a name. He can be known. In fact, he so wants to be known that he took on human flesh to prove it, to prove to us that he wants to be in relationship with us. Furthermore, the God who will be born to us at Christmas is a God who is not dated or merely "historical." He is not far away, a character in a story from two thousand years ago. He is alive *now*. He is moving now. He is active now. He is involved in your life now.

We should never ask, What would Jesus do? as if Jesus were dead forever or merely someone who lived two thousand years ago. We do not have to speculate or figure out what Jesus would do. There is good news for you! We can merely ask, Jesus, what *are* you doing now? God is active in *your* life *now*, and he only wants what is best for you. What he can provide for you is infinitely better than what you can provide for yourself.

For your prayer

Begin by reading Psalm 136. Notice in the Psalm how active God is. Beg the Lord that you may see him active in your life *now*, just as he was in the life of the psalmist.

"Father, help me to see you active and alive, now in the present moment. Provide for me in ways that are far more than I could ever ask or imagine."

What words stood out to you as you prayed? What did you find stirring in your heart?

for This mercy
endures forever

Whatever goes on,
god is there
w/ His mercy

DIFFERENT

"
Trust in the LORD
with all your heart.
"

—Proverbs 3:5

ELIZABETH

Elizabeth was the wife of Zechariah and the mother of John the Baptist. She was also a relative of Mary. Her relationship to Mary is not specified; however, Mary's respect for her was profound enough to inspire Mary, when she learned that Elizabeth was pregnant, to leave in haste and travel ninety miles for an extended visit (see Luke 1:39). For many years, Elizabeth prayed for a child, but the Bible tells us that she remained childless until very late in her life. As Elizabeth prayed for the miracle of a child, she had to remain patient as she waited for this prayer to be granted. Elizabeth would indeed give birth to John. Her prayer would be answered, for God wanted only what was best for her. However, her prayer would be answered in ways that were not what she expected. God wanted only what was best for her, but what was best for her was different from what Elizabeth imagined.

This week, I have asked you to consider whether you believe that God wants only what is best for you. On Sunday, I encouraged you to consider whether you are attached to particular outcomes. I did so because many of us think that the *way* we want our prayer to be answered is going to be *the way* we experience happiness. When we do this, we unknowingly "determine" what will make us happy. The danger here is that if God does not provide the outcome we want, then we may mistakenly conclude that God does not want what is best for us. That is why surrendering our outcomes, and offering them to God, is so important. God does want only what is best for you, and he can provide more for you than you can provide for yourself. But this might look very different than you think. Let us imagine that you are asking God for something, but let us say that what is *really* underneath the asking is a desire to be happy. So, in a sense, we think we are saying, "God, I want this." But, in reality, we are saying, "God, I want this *so that I can be happy*." God hears "I want this," but God also hears "so that I can be happy." Many times, what God provides for us is different from what we initially ask for because he ultimately answers the deeper longing—the longing to be happy in this example. God will provide. But sometimes it is just different from what we ask for.

For your prayer

Read Proverbs 3:5-6. Consider how Elizabeth would have prayed with the very words you are reading. Today, pray this prayer of St. Ignatius of Loyola. Set the alarms on your phone. Pray the prayer every three hours, at least at 9 AM, noon, 3 PM, 6 PM, and 9 PM. Ask for these words to penetrate your mind and heart:

"Take, Lord, and receive all my liberty, my memory, my understanding, and my entire will, all I have and call my own. You have given all to me. To you, Lord, I return it. Everything is yours; do with it what you will. Give me only your love and your grace. That is enough for me. Amen."[1]

I want to get to this point

What words stood out to you as you prayed?
What did you find stirring in your heart?

*words good but
the reality
of actually saying
a thing it is
something else*

WAIT

> "Our soul waits for the LORD; he is our help and shield."
>
> **—Psalm 33:20**

SIMEON

During the first Advent, Simeon was one of many in Israel who were praying and yearning for the Messiah. We meet him eight days after Jesus' birth at the Presentation in the Temple, but Simeon had surely been waiting for God to send his salvation for many, many years.

Luke's Gospel reads, "Now there was a man in Jerusalem, whose name was Simeon, and this man was righteous and devout, looking for the consolation of Israel, and the Holy Spirit was upon him. And it had been revealed to him by the Holy Spirit that he should not see death before he had seen the Lord's Christ" (Luke 2:25-26). Simeon was waiting for the Lord; he was waiting for the fulfillment of the promise made to him. What can we learn from Simeon? Many times, we have to wait for God to provide what was promised to us. God wants only what is best for us, and what God can provide for us is infinitely better than what we can provide for ourselves. However, what, how, or when God provides might look very different from what we expect, and often we have to wait on the provision. Waiting avails us of three particular graces. First, waiting purifies our desires. As I mentioned yesterday, there are often deeper desires "underneath" what we first ask for. *If we are attentive to our hearts during the waiting,* we often discover what we really want "underneath" what we first asked for. Thus, the waiting has a purpose: It is meant to draw us deeper into our hearts. God knows the deepest longing in the first asking. In making us wait, he is intentionally taking us deeper into self-awareness.

Second, waiting purifies our receptivity. *If we are attentive to our hearts during the waiting,* we often discover that we are more attached to specific outcomes than we first thought. The process of waiting can reveal our attachments. Thus, if we are praying during the wait, we may grow in the act of surrender. Once we surrender our attachments, we are more disposed to receive all that God wants to give to us. Third, waiting gives God time to work in other people's lives. Let us say, for example, that you are asking God for a miracle in your marriage or in the life of a family member, or maybe you are asking him to restore a relationship with someone you love dearly. In order for God to give you the gift, he may have to work a similar miracle in the other person's life. Not only does waiting do something in your life, but often God's blessings are bestowed in the process. Just as you have to cooperate with what God wants to do in your life, other people have to do the same. Thus, sometimes you might be ready to receive the gift, but other people might not be ready. That is when the waiting may lead us to intercession, and sometimes our experience of interceding for others can be part of the blessing God wants to give to us in our waiting.

For your prayer

Begin by reading Psalm 33. Today, consider the last time you had to wait for what you wanted or the last time you had to wait on the Lord. Look above at the three graces that we receive when we wait. Ask God to reveal to you why you were waiting.

"Father, help me to trust you and surrender to you. Help me to be patient and wait with you when I am waiting for you to answer a prayer."

What words stood out to you as you prayed?
What did you find stirring in your heart?

_____

_____

_____

_____

_____

_____

_____

_____

_____

_____

_____

_____

_____

_____

_____

_____

_____

_____

_____

_____

_____

_____

STAY

> "You are my help and
> my deliverer; do not
> delay, O my God!"

—Psalm 40:17

ANNA

Another person was praying and yearning for the Messiah before Jesus' birth—Anna. Like Simeon, she would finally see the joyous answer to her prayer when Mary and Joseph brought the baby to the Temple after his birth.

Luke tells us that "there was a prophetess, Anna, the daughter of Phan'uel, of the tribe of Asher; she was of a great age, having lived with her husband seven years from her virginity, and as a widow till she was eighty-four. She did not depart from the temple, worshiping with fasting and prayer night and day" (Luke 2:36-37). When she saw the baby Jesus with his parents, "coming up at that very hour she gave thanks to God, and spoke of him to all who were looking for the redemption of Jerusalem" (Luke 2:38).

Anna, too, was waiting for the Lord during the first Advent. We meet her eight days after Jesus' birth, but she had surely been waiting long before that. What can we learn from Anna? Anna was in the Temple the day Mary and Joseph brought Jesus there for his Presentation. We know she was there because Scripture says, "She did not depart from the temple, worshiping with fasting and prayer night and day." Because she was there, she beheld the person she was waiting for, namely, Jesus. She did not depart from the Temple. She never left. She *stayed* in the Temple. And, because she stayed, she received the gift she was yearning for. Anna teaches us to never leave, to *stay still* as we wait.

As a spiritual director, I often ask directees, "How do you feel about waiting?" Perhaps what I'm really asking is, "How long can you wait until you get tired of waiting and leave the posture of waiting so as to make things happen on your own?"

The temptation while waiting is to leave. The longer we wait on God, the more we will experience the tempting taunts that plant seeds of doubt. As we wait for the Lord to answer our prayer, we may be tempted to believe that God is not listening or that he is not acting or will not act. We may even be tempted to believe that God will not provide. Or, worse yet, we may be tempted to believe that the reason God is not acting is because we are doing something wrong. So, instead of staying interiorly still, we are tempted to take control and provide for ourselves what we think God is not providing for us.

Let us learn from Anna. "She did not depart from the temple." Also notice that she did not just stay in the Temple; she stayed engaged with God, "worshiping with fasting and prayer night and day." When we are waiting on the Lord, it is imperative that we do only what God tells us to do. Our Christian faith tells us that God is active and alive. Thus, we are to believe that God will provide. At the same time, we are to *actively* receive. This means that while we wait for God to act, we are to *do* something—we are to pray, listen, and do only what he tells us to do. Learn from Anna. Stay in the waiting.

For your prayer

Begin by reading Psalm 40. Ask God to show you how long you usually wait until you get tired of waiting and leave the posture of waiting so as to make things happen on your own.

"Father, help me to trust you and surrender to you. Help me to stay still when I am waiting."

What words stood out to you as you prayed? What did you find stirring in your heart?

_____
_____
_____
_____
_____
_____
_____
_____
_____
_____
_____
_____
_____
_____
_____
_____
_____
_____
_____
_____
_____
_____
_____

TIMING

"My thoughts are not your thoughts, neither are your ways my ways, says the LORD."

—Isaiah 55:8

ASHER

Luke 2:36 states that Anna was "of the tribe of Asher." Who was Asher, and what can we learn from him? Asher was the eighth son of Abraham's grandson Jacob and father of one of the twelve tribes of Israel. Asher's name is derived from a word that means "to make or declare happy." The tribe of Asher was one of the northernmost tribes, which settled in the northwest corner of the northern kingdom, adjacent to the Mediterranean Sea. Asher's descendants were one of the ten "lost tribes" of Israel who were conquered by the Assyrian Empire in 722 BC and dispersed. A few northern Israelites avoided the exile by escaping to the southern kingdom of Judah, and it is thought that Anna's ancestors may have been among them. Anna's presence as a daughter of the tribe of Asher shows God's care even for the lost tribes who, because of their unfaithfulness, had been conquered. Isaiah prophesied that the lost tribes of Israel would be gathered together again by the Messiah (see Isaiah 11:10-16). So Anna, in the Temple, is awaiting the arrival of the Messiah for both herself and her people, who have been waiting for 722 years to be rescued by God.

Imagine waiting 722 years for God to answer your prayer! The timing of God's promise was not what Asher was expecting, and that is precisely what we can learn from this unique detail of the Advent story: God's timing is not our timing.

God does have timing. God wants only what is best for us, and what God can provide for us is infinitely better than what we can provide for ourselves. God knows not only *what* to give us but *when* to give it to us. His timing is not accidental. His timing coincides with when we are most able to receive his gift within the larger story of where he is leading us.

God's timing is also affected by our receptivity. There have been many times in my own life when God was ready to do something, but because of my immaturity, selfishness, or sinfulness I was not ready to receive it. God's timing may be delayed not because of his desires but because of our inability to let him act. Furthermore, God's timing may be affected by other people's resistance. As we saw on Thursday, we may be waiting on God because others are not ready to cooperate with his plan. It is really important that we remain honest with ourselves about how we feel about God's timing. Sometimes, we may grow frustrated or resentful because God's timing is not our own. It is then that the process of waiting reveals the subtleties of our heart and the attachments within it. That is why Anna can teach us so much: We must stay engaged as we wait and share with God *everything* in our hearts.

For your prayer

Begin by reading Isaiah 55:1-9. Look back on the second week of Advent. What were the themes? What did God say? What have you learned about yourself? What have you learned about God?

"Father, help me to trust you and surrender to you. Teach me about your timing, especially when your timing is not my timing."

What words stood out to you as you prayed?
What did you find stirring in your heart?

_____

_____

_____

_____

_____

_____

_____

_____

_____

_____

_____

_____

_____

_____

_____

_____

_____

_____

_____

The Third Week of Advent

Events

"Behold, I am doing a new thing; now it springs forth, do you not perceive it?"

—Isaiah 43:19

WHEN WE THINK

of Advent, we most easily think of the events that have become such a part of our Christian imagination: Mary's Annunciation, the dream of the angel that reversed Joseph's decision to divorce Mary, the census, and the pilgrimage to Bethlehem with "no place for them in the inn" (Luke 2:7). These events, and others that we shall see, were quite dramatic. They reveal much to us about God and just how far he will go to reveal the beauty of his heart.

Welcome to the third week of Advent. This week we shall learn more about how these events shaped the reality of the very first Advent.

DESIRE

"God ... breathed

into his nostrils the

breath of life; and man

became a living soul."

—**Genesis 2:7**

MARY'S ANNUNCIATION

There can be no mention of Advent without the Annunciation, for it was in Gabriel's visit to Mary that the Blessed Mother conceived the Christ-child within her. Several details of Luke 1:26-38 are most familiar. We recall that Mary was a virgin. We remember that she asked, "How can this be?" since she had no husband. Perhaps most famous is her great *fiat*, the moment of her yes to the Lord. All these details are common in the Christian imagination.

However, there is one detail that is mentioned before all the others but is easily missed. The Bible says, "In the sixth month the angel Gabriel was *sent from God* to a city of Galilee named Nazareth, to a virgin betrothed to a man whose name was Joseph, of the house of David; and the virgin's name was Mary" (Luke 1:26-27; emphasis added). Let us look at the words "sent from God." *God* did this. God took the initiative.

With all the beautiful honor attributed to Our Lady, may I, with great reverence, respect, and humility, remind us that the Annunciation is much less about Mary and much more about God—and the event reveals much about him. Most importantly, it reveals *God's deep desire to be a part of our lives.*

God is relationship; he is desire itself. In the very beginning, in Genesis 1, we read that God created the heavens and the earth. Why? God did not create because he had to, for God existed for all of eternity without creation. God created because he wanted to. And God did not create man because he had to. God created Adam and Eve because he desired, he wanted, to be known.

Let us continue with the story of salvation. God formed a covenant with Abraham because he wanted to. He chose Israel as his own because he wanted to. He sent the prophets and led the Israelites before, during, and after the Exile because he wanted to.

There is one reason why we will celebrate Christmas, and one reason why we are preparing for Jesus' birth during Advent—because God wanted it. *God took on flesh because he wanted to.* God chose to be born because he wanted to. God chose to come to Mary because he wanted to. None of

this was because he needed to. It is all because he wanted to.

When you are wondering if God wants what is best for you, remember this: *God desires you.* When you are wondering if God can provide more for you, remember this: God desires you. When you are wondering if you should wait on God, remember this: God desires you.

You were not conceived or created because God needed you. You are alive because God desires you. Let that soak in: You are desired by God.

For your prayer

Begin by reading Genesis 1:1–2:7. Consider the fact that you are not needed but wanted. After you read the Scriptures, listen to the song "Through and Through" by Will Reagan.[2] Consider the fact that you are alive because God wants to be known by you.

"Father, take me deep within. Help me to personally experience your desire for me."

What words stood out to you as you prayed?
What did you find stirring in your heart?

That I am
desired by God -
how Wonderful

With all my sins +
Character Flaws -
God loves me!

PEOPLE

"A faithful friend is a sturdy shelter: he that has found one has found a treasure."

—Sirach 6:14

VISITATION

The first major event of Advent immediately leads to the next event: the Visitation. Luke's Gospel states, "In those days Mary arose and went with haste into the hill country, to a city of Judah, and she entered the house of Zechari'ah and greeted Elizabeth" (Luke 1:39-40). Mary left in haste because she wanted to see Elizabeth. The angel had told Mary that Elizabeth was six months pregnant and would also bear a son. Elizabeth was Mary's kinswoman and much older, maybe an aunt or cousin or sister-in-law. Her pregnancy, too, was a miracle. Mary was surely eager to see Elizabeth to be of help to her in the last months of pregnancy. But Mary also needed Elizabeth. She needed to share God's goodness, the news of her own pregnancy and all that was in her heart, with someone who understood—someone who could understand the miracle and the reality of who she was carrying in her womb. With her heart filled with emotion, Mary visits Elizabeth.

What we learn from the Visitation is that we all need people. We are not meant to walk the journey alone. Mary needed Joseph. Mary needed Elizabeth. She needed other people to be with her throughout her life. If the Blessed Mother, who was born without original sin, needed other people, how much more do you and I need other people to help us in our relationship with God. The mere fact that you are reading this book during Advent, and still reading this book three weeks into Advent, is a simple sign that you, too, need people in your life. This Advent companion in many ways is just that, a companion insofar as you and I are walking together through the text of each day's meditations. Isn't that why we pick up books like this, because we know we need help in our relationship with God? But as good as books, videos, and podcasts are, we need real people, in the flesh, that we can lean on in the tough times. In fact, I will make a bet with you. Look back on the times in your life when you flourished in your relationship with God, and I will bet that you had someone who was helping you in some way. And I will make another bet with you. Look back on the times in your life when you struggled in your relationship with God, and I will bet that those were the moments when you were isolated from healthy relationships or were tempted away from healthy relationships.

To be in relationship is to be human. However, those relationships are even more important when we are struggling with all that we discussed last week, including doubt, outcomes different from what we expected, long stretches of waiting, and surprising timing.

As you look back on your reflections from week one, perhaps reconsider what you really want at this stage of life. Do you have someone or some ones who you can lean on in the tough times? Is that something that you need to ask the Lord to provide? Spend some time in prayer today, and think about the people you have or need in your life.

For your prayer

Begin by reading Sirach 6:5-17. Consider how often Mary would have prayed with these very same words. What is God saying to you in the Bible passage? Specifically, what is God saying to you about people?

"Father, reveal to me the people you have placed in my life who can help me in my relationship with you."

What words stood out to you as you prayed?
What did you find stirring in your heart?

I have a friend
who is the
type who is a
friend when it
suits her.
Do I tolerate her
or drop her?
What would
Jesus do?

Does she fear
God as I do?

REVERENCE

" You are
precious in my
eyes, and honored,
and I love you. **"**

—Isaiah 43:4

JOSEPH'S ANNUNCIATION

The angel Gabriel visited Mary during her Annunciation, but Mary was not the only person to receive a visit from Gabriel with life-changing news. Matthew tells us the story of Joseph's annunciation: "When [Jesus'] mother Mary had been betrothed to Joseph, before they came together she was found to be with child of the Holy Spirit; and her husband Joseph, being a just man and unwilling to put her to shame, resolved to send her away quietly. But as he considered this, behold, an angel of the Lord appeared to him in a dream" (Matthew 1:18-20).

The news of Mary's conception must have affected Joseph deeply. While we are uncertain about the exact reasons for his decision to divorce her quietly, we can easily presume that whatever his interior struggles were, they were enough to cause Joseph to alter his plans with the Blessed Mother. Joseph was struggling with the unexpectancies of life, and never did he need God more than he did at this moment. The beauty of Joseph's annunciation is that God met Joseph where Joseph was. God reverenced Joseph's struggle, and, instead of expecting Joseph to be someone that he was not, God met him where he was, precisely *in* the struggle.

What we learn from the event of Joseph's annunciation is that God always meets us where we are rather than where we think we need to be. God reverences where we are in life, and, from that place of where we are, God begins ever anew his relationship with us.

When we doubt or wait, God meets us where we are. When we struggle with different outcomes or timing, God meets us where we are. When we struggle to believe that God wants only what is best for us, God meets us where we are. And, when we struggle to believe that God can provide for us something better than we can provide for ourselves, God meets us where we are. Today's meditation finds us in the third week of Advent. Perhaps your Advent thus far has been filled with grace, and your daily consistency with these meditations has been perfect. If that is where you are, great. Thank the Lord for the blessing. For others of us, maybe this Advent has not met our expectations. Maybe life has gotten in the way of your consistency in prayer. Or perhaps things have surfaced in your heart during this Advent that you either did not expect or do not feel comfortable with. Wherever you are today, that is okay. It is where you are. It is here, where you are in reality, that God is going to meet you.

God meets us where we are but loves us too much to leave us there. God is always asking us to take a step closer to him, regardless of where we are when we take that first step. Ask God to meet you in the present moment, regardless of where you are or think you should be.

For your prayer

Begin by reading Isaiah 43:1-7. Consider how often Joseph would have prayed with these very same words. What is God saying to you in the Bible passage? Specifically, what is God saying to you about how he sees you?

"Father, help me to find you with me where I am rather than where I think I need to be."

What words stood out to you as you prayed?
What did you find stirring in your heart?

God calls me
by name; I am His

He is my
protector

SURPRISES

"[The LORD] heals
the brokenhearted,
and binds up
their wounds.

—Psalm 147:3"

CENSUS

One of the things that I find fascinating about the Advent story is the brilliant way that God uses surprises and unexpected news to reveal his glory. Mary's Annunciation and the conceiving of Jesus were a surprise, to say the least. Mary was not expecting this. Elizabeth's conceiving of John the Baptist at a late age was another dramatic surprise. Zechariah and Elizabeth were not expecting this. For Joseph too, Mary's pregnancy was a shocking surprise. Joseph was not expecting this. Angels brought messages with life-changing news. Zechariah was struck mute. John the Baptist leapt in his mother's womb. The Advent story is one surprise after another.

And then came the news of the census. Just when they thought that the dramatic twists were over, "a decree went out from Caesar Augustus that all the world should be enrolled" (Luke 2:1). Eight months into Mary's pregnancy, but without an exact date for the expected birth of her son, Mary and Joseph had to once again adjust to a surprise. News of the census would have been a shock to everyone. It required hundreds of thousands of people throughout Israel to leave their homes and return to the cities of their ancestors to be counted. What we learn from the event of the census is that God can use the surprises of life for his glory. Remember our meditation on the Saturday of the first week of Advent? The birth of the Messiah in Bethlehem was necessary for the fulfillment of the Old Testament prophecies. While news of the census was a surprise to Mary and Joseph, it was not a surprise to God. God was prepared to use this surprise to fulfill what he had promised long ago.

The surprises of life catch us off guard, for that is the nature of surprises. The surprises of life do not fit inside our neatly packaged plans, ideals, or efforts to control our lives. Some of the surprises in life affect us personally, while other surprises affect those whom we love deeply. Some of these surprises profoundly alter our physical health, emotional stability, work, finances, or even life itself.

Perhaps no other time of the year is so filled with surprises as is December. There may be surprises in what we experience in our preparations for Christmas or the celebration itself. There may be surprises with family, with who does or does not show up, or with how events actually unfold. We may also be surprised by our emotions, whether it be how we feel about how things unfold or how we feel about the holidays in general.

Remember this: Surprises are part of life, and God can use every surprise for his glory. The key is to stay in a relationship with God. Ask the Lord what he is doing in your life in the midst of the surprise.

For your prayer

Begin by reading Psalm 147. Consider how often Mary and Joseph would have prayed with these very same words. Listen to the Psalm as it speaks of how God provides in every circumstance, regardless of the surprise.

"Father, help me to trust you, no matter what surprises may come my way."

What words stood out to you as you prayed?
What did you find stirring in your heart?

— God heals the
broken hearted &
— sustains the
lonely
— Calls us by name
— Provides for us

Why Worry?

HARD

> " I will protect him,
> because he knows
> my name. "
>
> **—Psalm 91:14**

PILGRIMAGE

Another thing that I find fascinating with the Advent story is the extraordinary hardship that was a part of the lives of those we have come to learn about. Let us revisit what we discussed during the first two weeks of this Advent. In week one, we read about Herod's palace. The occupation of the Romans, and the brutality of their rule, would have made life very hard for God's Chosen People. In week two, we read about the generosity of Joachim and Anne and their offering Mary to the Lord and her growing up in the Temple. How they must have missed her—missing out on many of the key moments of her life. It would also have been difficult for Zechariah and Elizabeth to be childless for so many years. Children were a sign of God's blessing. For Zechariah, who was a priest in the Temple and a man of great prestige, it would have been hard to not have children as a sign of God's blessing.

Let us not forget that during the first Advent, life was hard. Now, let us consider the surprises of Advent. Specifically, the surprise of the census required Mary and Joseph to journey ninety miles south to Bethlehem. Mary's pregnancy and Joseph's meager income would have made that journey much more difficult than we imagine.

What we learn from the pilgrimage to Bethlehem is that sometimes life is hard. However, just as God can use the surprises for his glory, so God can do great things when life is hard. Let us recall what we talked about last week. Letting go of control and outcomes can be hard. Doubt can be hard, and most of us doubt God when the circumstances we are facing are hard. Waiting on God can be hard. Unmet expectations can be hard.

Staying engaged with God when life is difficult can be hard. Accepting God's timing can be hard.

One of the interesting aspects of the secular Christmas season is its attempt to mask the difficulties of life. The lights and parties, presents and music—everything we call "the Christmas spirit"—don't make the hardships go away. They just mask them with decorations.

 Now, here is the good news. God chose to be born in the midst of all that was hard. When God entered the human story at the time and in the place he did, he willingly entered into the hardship that was a part of that time and those places. God is not afraid of "hard." He entered what was hard so that we might forever know that he is *with* us precisely *in* what is hard.

Listen to me: You are not alone, especially where your life is hard. The baby we are waiting for will be named Emmanuel, which means "God is with us." He is *with* you precisely where it is hard.

For your prayer

Begin by reading Psalm 91. Consider how often Mary and Joseph would have prayed these very same words. Listen to the Psalm as it speaks of how God is with us in what is hard in our lives.

"Father, help me to find you with me, especially when and where life seems hard."

What words stood out to you as you prayed?
What did you find stirring in your heart?

ROOM

"Create in me a clean
heart, O God."

—Psalm 51:10

INN

On Wednesday, we talked about surprises, and, yesterday, we spoke about what is hard. Imagine what it was like for Mary and Joseph as they arrived in Bethlehem: "And Joseph also went up from Galilee, from the city of Nazareth, to Judea, to the city of David, which is called Bethlehem, because he was of the house and lineage of David, to be enrolled with Mary his betrothed, who was with child. And while they were there, the time came for her to be delivered. And she gave birth to her first-born son and wrapped him in swaddling cloths, and laid him in a manger, because there was no place for them in the inn" (Luke 2:4-7).

There was no room. After walking ninety long miles, they were told there was no room. Knowing that Mary was to give birth at any minute but not knowing when or where, they were told there was no room. Trusting that God had led them to Bethlehem, the first thing they heard was that there was no room.

What we learn from their reception in Bethlehem is that now is the time to make room in our "inn." Now is the time for us to make room for the One we are preparing for. In a very real way, God does not want to be born in Bethlehem or some far off city. This Christmas, Christ wants to be born in your heart.

Today is a good time for us to talk about two things that you can do to make room in your heart so that this Christmas might be deeply personal and perhaps even life-changing.

The first thing you can do is consider celebrating the sacrament of Reconciliation. Many of us are in the habit of going to confession twice a year, at Easter and at Christmas. If this is you, I invite you to go deeper this year with a more thorough examination of conscience. For some readers, it may have been quite a long time since you last went to confession. Whether it is because you have theological questions about confessing your sins to a Catholic priest or because of a sense of shame or guilt, may I simply invite you to ask the Lord what he desires for you this Christmas. In fact, let me be more blunt. I would ask that *you* not make the decision about confession. Ask the Lord to make the decision, and have the courage to do whatever he tells you to do.

2. The second thing you may consider in order to make room in your heart is to forgive one person who is in most need of mercy. I once heard it said that they only call it mercy when you do not deserve it. Do not wait for them to deserve your forgiveness—that is precisely why they call it mercy. There may be someone in your life now or someone you will see next week who needs your forgiveness. Ask the Lord to show you what he sees.

For your prayer

Begin by reading Psalm 51. Listen to the words of the Psalm and have the courage to be honest with yourself about where you are with sin.

"Father, help me to trust you and surrender to you. Reveal to me where I am most in need of forgiveness and mercy."

What words stood out to you as you prayed?
What did you find stirring in your heart?

_____

_____

_____

_____

_____

_____

_____

_____

_____

_____

_____

_____

_____

_____

_____

_____

_____

_____

_____

_____

_____

_____

HUMBLE

"My soul thirsts for you."

—Psalm 63:1

MANGER

With no room for them in the inn, and, therefore, no room for them in Bethlehem, Mary and Joseph headed for the outskirts of the city in search of a place for Jesus' birth. Tradition has long held that Jesus was born on the outskirts of the city in a cave.

Jesus was not born in a fancy hospital or other pristine environment. Jesus was born in a humble cave where the animals lived.

What we learn from Mary and Joseph finding the cave is this: God chose a humble place for his birth, for God loves *humility*. Likewise, as we continue the conversation that we began yesterday, if this Christmas is going to be personal and perhaps even life-changing, we must begin now to look inside our hearts and ask for the grace of *humility*.

Regarding humility, may I ask you to be honest as you ask yourself, Do you *really* need a *Savior?* In my experience as a priest for over twenty years, Christmas remains an event that most of us look at from the outside in, an event that happened in the past. I can only imagine that one of the things that creates such a posture is our comfort and quality of self-provision—our desire to provide for ourselves. In other words, at this time of year, when we are preparing to host elaborate family gatherings and are piling presents under a tree, we may not feel that we really need a Savior. After all, we have what we want and what we think we need. Do we *really* need a God to *save* us?

Mary and Joseph knew that they needed God. Their humility was such that their hearts were open to receiving the *reality* of what God was trying to do at Christmas. If we do not feel that we *really* need a *Savior*, then the person born to us at Christmas will always be a little baby. And, after his birth, we will simply go back to our comfortable lives, which do not necessarily express a *need* for God.

Why do we need a Savior and not just a baby? When I have the humility to admit that I am a sinner, then I need a Savior. When I have the humility to admit that I cannot forgive my sins myself, then I need a Savior.

But there is more. Western Christianity has lost its sense of judgment and salvation. I cannot tell you how many times I have thought, said, or heard things like "Doesn't everyone get to heaven?" It is an uncomfortable question. To even consider the possibility that not everyone gets to heaven makes many of us personally uncomfortable. So either we don't think about it, or we go back to living a superficial life adorned in materialism.

I cannot think of any more important question that a person could ever ask or grapple with than the question of eternal salvation. After all, if I am wrong about the weather or who is going to win the Super Bowl, my life is not dramatically affected. But what happens if I get salvation wrong? There are not simply consequences to this question; there are eternal implications. *Forever.*

Furthermore, for those reading who are parents, your answer to the question of salvation may not only affect you eternally, but it may also affect the souls of your spouse and children. And I shudder to imagine what would be in someone's heart when they realize that their eternal salvation, as well as the eternal salvation of their spouse and children, was in jeopardy because they simply assumed that "everyone gets to heaven, don't they?"

The good news is that a Savior is given to us this Christmas. The good news is that eternal salvation is available to us if we have the courage to accept the gift of a Savior, not just a baby, this Christmas. As a priest of Jesus Christ, and as one who has had the privilege of walking with you for the past three weeks, I beg you to ask yourself if you really *need* a Savior. And I beg you to ask for the courage to answer the question with humility.

We have one week left to make room for him. We have one week left to prepare for his birth. Let us be reminded today that we are not making room for a baby. We are not preparing for a child. A Savior will be born for us. The question is, Do you *need* one?

For your prayer

Begin by reading Psalm 63. As you pray with the words of the Psalm, ask yourself, Am I ready for the Savior? Do I really need a Savior?

"Father, I beg you for the grace of humility.
Help me to see clearly how and where in my life I am in most need of a Savior."

What words stood out to you as you prayed?
What did you find stirring in your heart?

_____

_____

_____

_____

_____

_____

_____

_____

_____

_____

_____

_____

_____

_____

_____

_____

_____

_____

_____

_____

_____

NEED

"I will lift up my hands and call on your name. … [F]or you have been my help."

—Psalms 63:4,7

The Fourth Week of Advent

Open Hearts

"For you shall go out in joy, and be led forth in peace; the mountains … shall break forth into singing."

—Isaiah 55:12

THIS FINAL WEEK

of Advent is a little different from the first three weeks. The meditations shift from considering the people, places, and events of the first Advent to guided imaginative prayer with Mary and Joseph. The guided prayers are designed to help you open your heart to the Christ-child as you prepare for Christmas in a more personal way. In his book *Meditation and Contemplation,* Fr. Tim Gallagher, OMV, describes imaginative prayer in the method taught by St. Ignatius as imaginatively seeing the people in the Scripture passage, hearing their words as they speak, and observing their actions as they accomplish the event. It is a time-tested way of drawing closer to the Lord.

This week, I invite you to personally enter into each of the guided meditations. Be *in* the scene. Be *with* the people there. Once the scene comes to its natural conclusion, when you feel God moving you along, simply share your heart with the Lord.

YES

"Do not be afraid …

for you have found

favor with God."

—Luke 1:30

MARY RESPONDS TO GOD

Let us ask the Holy Spirit to help us imagine Mary's Annunciation. Let us imagine the home of Joachim and Anne, the home where Mary lives in Nazareth. Their house is simple, as are all the homes in Nazareth. Mary has risen early this morning to give the first hour of her day to the Lord in prayer. Today, as she does every day, Mary begins her morning prayer by singing the words of Psalm 51:17: "LORD, you will open my lips; and my mouth will proclaim your praise" (NAB).

Mary loves to sing, and singing the psalms brings her great joy. Her daily routine is to sing a few psalms in praise of God, and her singing eventually draws her into silence. This morning, however, she senses something is different. After singing the words of Psalm 51, she is immediately embraced by silence. She is still and expectant, for Mary loves silence and contemplation. Suddenly, a radiant light dawns in the tiny room in her home. Magnificent in radiance, the light is overwhelming in its purity and holiness. Mary does not know what is happening, but she is aware that something extraordinary is unfolding, and she knows she is in the presence of God. As the light surrounds her, Mary is aware of the presence of the angel Gabriel within the light. As Gabriel's greeting pierces Mary's heart—"Hail, full of grace, the Lord is with you!" (Luke 1:28)—she is filled with both humility and awe, but she is also troubled by his words. What can they mean? The light surrounding Mary shimmers with each word the angel speaks.

As the conversation between Mary and the angel unfolds, Mary's humility is overwhelmed by the awesome wonder of being chosen by God to be the mother of his Son. As Mary considers the invitation, she is confused by how it will come to be. But her attention quickly shifts from the "how" to the "who." As she casts all her focus on the Lord, she is calmed by the One who is asking.

Wholly absorbed in God, Mary's yes flows naturally from her heart, for she has always done whatever the Lord has asked of her. Mary's surrender to God today is not a new posture for her. Daily, in her prayer, Mary has said the very words she says now to Gabriel: "Behold, I am the handmaid of the Lord; let it be to me according to your word" (Luke 1:38).

Soon the angel departs, and the brilliant light gently fades away. Mary instinctively kneels in homage to the King of Kings, the child who is now in her womb. With her hands gently resting there, she sings the opening words of Psalm 98: "Sing a new song to the LORD, for he has done marvelous deeds" (NAB).

For your prayer

Find some time today to be alone. Find a quiet space. Slow down. Settle your heart. Close your eyes, and ask the Holy Spirit to inspire your imagination and guide you as you pray. Imagine the scene above. Be *in* the scene. Be *with* Mary as the angel Gabriel announces the news of the Incarnation.

What <u>words stood out</u> to you as you prayed?
What did you find stirring in your heart?

That Mary was
"favored" &
named so by
the angel

JOY

"The child in my womb
leaped for joy."

—Luke 1:44

MARY VISITS ELIZABETH

Let us ask the Holy Spirit to help us imagine the Visitation. The angel told Mary about Elizabeth's pregnancy, and now Mary leaves in haste, traveling south to Judah to see Elizabeth (see Luke 1:39). Mary is radiant, with a soft glow about her from the divine life that is within her. Her smile when she assented to the Lord's will has not left her face. Throughout the journey, quiet songs rise from her heart. As Mary leaves the caravan that she has traveled with, she enters the neighborhood of her extended family, knowing by memory the way to the home of Zechariah and Elizabeth. With excitement, she enters their home and sees Elizabeth, who is facing a window, her back to Mary. Mary giggles at the sight of her cousin and sings the words of the prophet Isaiah: "My people will abide in a peaceful habitation, in secure dwellings, and in quiet resting places" (Isaiah 32:18).

A surge of joy takes Elizabeth's breath away as her unborn son stirs. From her womb, John the Baptist has recognized the Messiah in Mary's womb. The stirring feels as if the child is dancing. In a fraction of a second, Elizabeth's thoughts are of the great King David, who "danced before the LORD with all his might" (2 Samuel 6:14) when the Ark of the Covenant was brought to his home in Jerusalem.

Elizabeth's eyes fill with joyful tears as she turns in awe to the sound of Mary's voice. Elizabeth falls to her knees in homage as she understands instantly that the Ark of the New Covenant is now in her home. As she kneels, it feels as if John the Baptist is reaching toward Jesus to touch him. Elizabeth is overcome, and, filled with the Holy Spirit, she exclaims with a loud cry, "Blessed are you among women, and blessed is the fruit of your womb!" (Luke 1:42).

Mary steps forward to Elizabeth, who is still kneeling. Transfixed as if in Eucharistic Adoration, Elizabeth places her hands on Mary's abdomen and begins to weep with joy. Mary's own heart is full. Her voice makes manifest the joy of her heart as she sings her Magnificat. Her opening words, "My soul magnifies the Lord, and my spirit rejoices in God my Savior" (Luke 1:46-47), fill the home as if a choir of angels were singing in triumph. Mary takes Elizabeth's hands, and the two women hug in an embrace confirming the words that poured forth from Mary's lips: "For he who is mighty has done great things for me, and holy is his name" (Luke 1:49).

For your prayer

Find some time today to be alone. Find a quiet space. Slow down. Settle your heart. Close your eyes, and ask the Holy Spirit to inspire your imagination and guide you as you pray. Imagine the scene above. Be *in* the scene. Be *with* Mary and be *with* Elizabeth in all that is sacred in their encounter.

What words stood out to you as you prayed?
What did you find stirring in your heart?

_____

_____

_____

_____

_____

_____

_____

_____

_____

_____

_____

_____

_____

_____

_____

_____

_____

_____

_____

_____

_____

Fourth Week — MEDITATION TWO

WITH

" My shield is
with God. "

—Psalm 7:10

MARY RETURNS TO NAZARETH

Let us ask the Holy Spirit to help us imagine Mary's return to Nazareth after the Visitation. It took Mary ten days to travel south to see Elizabeth, and Luke tells us that "Mary remained with her about three months, and returned to her home" (Luke 1:56). So it is now almost four months since Mary conceived the child. Scripture does not tell us if she has told Joseph or her parents yet.

Let us ask the Holy Spirit to help us enter the scene. Mary's heart is filled with many emotions and questions as she journeys back to Nazareth. On the one hand, her memory is anchored in the Annunciation and the Visitation, in her encounter with Gabriel and her months with Elizabeth. Both extraordinary events have revealed the glory and power of God and the miracles that pour forth from his blessing. On the other hand, Mary needs to speak to her parents and to Joseph. How will she explain this to her parents? What will they say? How will they react? And how will she explain this to Joseph? Will he understand? What will be his response? And what about small-town Nazareth? Will there be gossip? What about her friends? Will others believe in the miracle? As Mary walks, her mind is crowded with thoughts that require faith in the Lord's providence.

As Mary feels the temptation of anxiety, she also feels the slight stirrings of the child within her and is again at peace. She recalls the words of the angel Gabriel: "For with God nothing will be impossible" (Luke 1:37). With her eyes fixed on the Lord's promises, Mary knows that as she prepares to speak to her parents and Joseph, *with* God nothing will be impossible. Mary is assured that even in small-town Nazareth nothing will be impossible *with God.*

Mary's journey back to Nazareth is now almost done. As she looks down the hill on the tiny village that is home, many emotions flood her heart. And, as she reaches the outer edge of the village, she is reminded again that *with* God nothing will be impossible. *"With God"* will be her place of refuge. She will speak to her parents and Joseph *with God.* Now more than ever, Mary needs to do all things *with* God.

For your prayer

Find some time today to be alone. Find a quiet space. Slow down. Settle your heart. Close your eyes, and ask the Holy Spirit to inspire your imagination and guide you as you pray. Imagine the scene above. Be *in* the scene. Be *with* Mary. Be *with* Mary as she returns home to Nazareth.

What words stood out to you as you prayed?
What did you find stirring in your heart?

_____

_____

_____

_____

_____

_____

_____

_____

_____

_____

_____

_____

_____

_____

_____

_____

_____

_____

_____

_____

_____

_____

SURRENDER

"
The Lord himself will
give you a sign.

—Isaiah 7:14
"

JOSEPH
RESPONDS TO GOD

Let us ask the Holy Spirit to help us enter into Joseph's own annunciation. Mary has now told Joseph about the child she is carrying. She told him about the extraordinary visit of the angel Gabriel and what the angel said: The child "will be called the Son of the Most High. ... [He] will be called holy, the Son of God" (Luke 1:32, 35). Joseph was deeply moved by her words because he knew her so well, and he knew that she was at peace with God's plan. She was certain about all she experienced and confident that God would lead Joseph to understanding. Joseph begged God for guidance, praying to know the Lord's will.

Let us ask the Holy Spirit to help us enter into this experience. At first, Matthew tells us, Joseph resolved to end their betrothal and send Mary away quietly (see Matthew 1:19) so that she would not be shamed. But tonight, as Joseph sleeps, an angel appears to him in a dream. The angel says, "Joseph, son of David, do not fear to take Mary your wife, for that which is conceived in her is of the Holy Spirit; she will bear a son, and you shall call his name Jesus, for he will save his people from their sins" (Matthew 1:20-21). Joseph wakes now, trembling. His heart is pounding, but he is not afraid. He trusted that God would respond but did not expect that God would do so in such a clear and dramatic way. He rises from his bed and kneels in awe, overwhelmed by the power and the presence of the Lord. As the psalms are the substance of Joseph's daily prayer, the words of Psalm 118 now flow from his heart: "O give thanks to the LORD, for he is good; his mercy endures for ever! ... Out of my distress I called on the LORD; the LORD answered me and set me free" (Psalm 118:1, 5).

He slowly grasps the reality of what he knows is true. The Messiah, so long promised to Israel, so eagerly awaited, is now alive in the womb of his betrothed. With tears of joy, he pours out his heart to the Lord and surrenders himself wholly to him. Lifting his hands to heaven, he exclaims, "Give thanks to the LORD, invoke his name; make known among the peoples his deeds! Sing praise to him, play music; proclaim all his wondrous deeds! Glory in his holy name; let hearts that seek the LORD rejoice! Seek out the LORD and his might; constantly seek his face. Recall the wondrous deeds he has done, his wonders and words of judgment" (Psalm 105:1-5; NAB).

The emotions of the moment soon draw Joseph into silence. With great reverence, he thinks of Mary and the child she is carrying. And there, in the quiet, he hears the echo of the ancient prophecy that the angel repeated in his dream: "Behold, a virgin shall conceive and bear a son, and his name shall be called Emmanuel (which means, God with us)" (Matthew 1:23).

For your prayer

Find some time today to be alone. Find a quiet space. Slow down. Settle your heart. Close your eyes, and ask the Holy Spirit to inspire your imagination and guide you as you pray. Imagine the scene above. Be *in* the scene. Be *with* Joseph in this very sacred moment in his life.

What words stood out to you as you prayed? What did you find stirring in your heart?

_____

_____

_____

_____

_____

_____

_____

_____

_____

_____

_____

_____

_____

_____

_____

_____

_____

_____

_____

_____

_____

_____

_____

ALL

"I know that you can do all things, and that no purpose of yours can be thwarted."

—**Job 42:2**

JOSEPH AND MARY TRUST THE LORD

With joy, Joseph has taken Mary as his wife, and they have settled into the house he built for them. It is a modest house but beautiful in its way, with shelves and cupboards just where they are needed, a large table, and many places for family and friends to sit and talk. Mary is in the last weeks of her pregnancy now, and they are busy as they get ready for the birth. The news of the census comes as a shock to Joseph. In the village this morning, he learned that he and Mary must soon travel to Bethlehem, his ancestral home, to be counted by the Romans. But how can they travel now when Mary is so great with child? And how will they afford supplies for the ninety-mile journey?

Let us ask the Holy Spirit to help us enter into the scene as Joseph tells Mary about the census. Joseph prays for guidance, leaning on the Scriptures. And, as he prays, he is led to the words of the prophet Isaiah: "Fear not, for I am with you, be not dismayed, for I am your God; I will strengthen you, I will help you, I will uphold you with my victorious right hand" (Isaiah 41:10).

As Joseph enters their home, he kisses the mezuzah on the doorpost and repeats the *Shema* to himself. He thinks he is beginning to understand what God means when he says, "You shall love the Lord your God with *all* your heart, and with *all* your soul, and with *all* your might" (Deuteronomy 6:5; emphasis added). He is beginning to understand *all*. This journey to Bethlehem will take all Joseph can give. Mary sees that Joseph is troubled as he comes into the room. She pours cool water for them both and sits with him. He tells her about the census and the journey to Bethlehem.

Mary is surprised and dismayed, for, like Joseph, she trusts the Lord but cannot see how the journey is possible. They pray together as naturally as they talk. They have been quiet for several minutes when Joseph takes Mary's hands and lifts her up, smiling: "As the heavens are higher than the earth," he quotes, "so are my ways higher than your ways and my thoughts than your thoughts" (Isaiah 55:9). It is Isaiah again. Mary laughs and continues where he left off: "For as the rain and the snow come down from heaven, and do not return there but water the earth … so shall my word be that goes forth from my mouth; it shall not return to me empty, but it shall accomplish that which I intend, and prosper in the thing for which I sent it" (Isaiah 55:10-11).

They both know the line that follows—"For you shall go out in joy, and be led forth in peace" (Isaiah 55:12). They know now that this is how it will be, and they are not afraid of the journey they must make.

For your prayer

Find some time today to be alone. Find a quiet space. Slow down. Settle your heart. Close your eyes, and ask the Holy Spirit to inspire your imagination and guide you as you pray. Imagine the scene above. Be *in* the scene. Be *with* Mary and Joseph as they process the news of the census.

What words stood out to you as you prayed?
What did you find stirring in your heart?

That I must cling
with faith to God's
words in all the
noted scriptures like
Is 41:10
" Fear not for
I am with you ..."
No matter what comes
up in 2022 - that
is my motto (Fear not)
Not for money not
for high issues
not for sickness or
whatever!

PILGRIMAGE

> "I will greatly rejoice in the LORD, my soul shall exult in my God."
>
> **—Isaiah 61:10**

MARY REFLECTS

Let us ask the Holy Spirit to help us imagine Mary's experience of the journey to Bethlehem. So much of her experience of traveling to Bethlehem is shaped by the man who is leading her to the city of David. Joseph has always been a safe and trusted place for Mary to rest. She trusts Joseph more than she trusts anyone on earth. Mary has always felt free to be who she is because of Joseph's holiness. She, in her femininity, has always felt safe because of his purity, self-awareness, and mastery of his own heart. However, more than anything, Mary trusts Joseph's ability to hear the voice of God and his unwavering obedience, his ready willingness to do whatever God asks him to do.

Joseph, as a laborer and carpenter, does not have enough money to own a donkey, but the Lord provided one through the generosity of a neighbor. It means Mary can travel in a little comfort. As Mary rests on the donkey, she really rests in Joseph. Her unwavering trust in Joseph is such that Mary knows she does not have to worry about anything except the child within her. She trusts that Joseph knows where he is going, will keep them safe as they travel, and will tend to her needs even before she asks.

Because of her security in Joseph's maturity, Mary's thoughts are completely taken up with the child she is carrying. Throughout the long days of pilgrimage to Bethlehem, Mary often sings her favorite psalms. Jesus from within Mary's womb has grown to recognize the voice of his mother and often stirs at the sound of her singing. Joseph, who is walking just ahead of the donkey, often looks back at Mary to check on her. Mary's happiness radiates from her face as she sings.

So many people are traveling now because of the census. Mary studies the faces of the others in their group and in the groups they pass. She can sense their longing for the promised Messiah. As she beholds their faces and ponders the Scriptures, her heart is often moved to recall the sacred words of the prophet Isaiah: "The Spirit of the Lord GOD is upon me, because the LORD has anointed me to bring good tidings to the afflicted; he has sent me to bind up the brokenhearted, to proclaim liberty to the captives, and the opening of the prison to those who are bound; to proclaim the year of the LORD's favor, and the day of vengeance of our God; to comfort all who mourn" (Isaiah 61:1-2). As Mary whispers aloud the words of the prophet, Jesus stirs so suddenly in her womb that Mary has to catch her breath. It is then she is reminded that this pilgrimage to Bethlehem is about much more than the birth of her son. It is about the birth of the Savior.

For your prayer

Find some time today to be alone. Close your eyes, and ask the Holy Spirit to inspire your imagination and guide you as you pray. Imagine the scene above. Be *in* the scene. Be *with* Mary as she and Joseph travel to Bethlehem.

What words stood out to you as you prayed?
What did you find stirring in your heart?

_____

_____

_____

_____

_____

_____

_____

_____

_____

_____

_____

_____

_____

_____

_____

_____

_____

_____

_____

_____

_____

PROVIDE

"In your goodness,
O God, you provided
for the needy."

—Psalm 68:10

MARY PREPARES FOR JESUS' BIRTH

Let us ask the Holy Spirit to help us imagine Mary as she prepares to give birth to her son. As Joseph leads the donkey up the mountain to the city of Bethlehem, Mary can sense that the time for her to give birth is fast approaching. Genesis 3 outlines the consequences of original sin, with the pains of childbirth being one of them. Mary, born without original sin, would have a very different experience of childbirth than any other woman in history. But, while the signs of the approaching birth are different for her, she knows it is coming and begins to prepare.

With each step up the mountain, she and Joseph are one step closer to Bethlehem. Mary is grateful for the donkey that was provided for her; however, the constant swaying back and forth is simply uncomfortable for anyone, much less a woman as pregnant as Mary. She trusts that Joseph will find accommodations and that the Lord himself will provide a space for the birth of her son.

Imagine their surprise as they arrive in Bethlehem to find out that there is no room for them in the city. While this news would have deeply affected Joseph, and the masculine heart's desire to provide, the surprise lack of available space in Bethlehem is disappointing news for Mary. Both Mary and Joseph have absolute trust in God, and both of them look deep within their hearts for further clarity as to where to go for the birth. Mary has unwavering trust in Joseph's ability to hear the voice of the Lord. As Joseph tells her that they will head to the outskirts of the city, Mary nods her head in agreement and trust.

God has *provided* for Mary throughout her entire life. However, specifically, God has *provided* for Mary at every moment since the Annunciation. God *provided* confirmation of his miraculous power as Mary visited Elizabeth. God *provided* the words she needed when she shared the news with her parents and with Joseph. God *provided* her with patience and trust as she waited for Joseph to surrender to God's will after he resolved to divorce her quietly. God *provided* the angel to speak to Joseph so that he could offer his life to God just as Mary did in her Annunciation. God has *provided* for them every moment since they left Nazareth, and Mary is confident that God will *provide* for them at this hour of their need.

Mary is confident that God will *provide*. As Joseph eventually finds the place where she is to give birth, Mary is less focused on *what* has been provided and more focused on the fact that God *has* provided. She is focused on *who* will be born more than she is focused on *where* he will be born. God *has* provided, and Mary is ready.

For your prayer

Find some time today to be alone. Close your eyes, and ask the Holy Spirit to inspire your imagination and guide you as you pray. Imagine the scene above. Be *in* the scene. Be *with* Mary as she prepares to give birth to her son.

**What words stood out to you as you prayed?
What did you find stirring in your heart?**

_____

_____

_____

_____

_____

_____

_____

_____

_____

_____

_____

_____

_____

_____

_____

_____

_____

_____

_____

_____

_____

_____

_____

FACE

"Let your face shine on

your servant; save me in

your merciful love!"

—**Psalm 31:16**

CHRIST IS BORN

Let us ask the Holy Spirit to help us enter into the scene of the birth of Christ. God has provided a simple cave on the outskirts of Bethlehem, a humble place where animals have gathered. Let us imagine this setting as the chosen place for the birth of the Messiah.

Mary is lying on a blanket. Nearby is a feeding trough for the animals, which she has filled with clean straw and soft wool for the baby. Joseph sits beside her, speaking to her quietly and smoothing her hair. They have lit a small lamp, which sheds a gentle light on them both. As the birth approaches, Joseph speaks to Mary quietly. He reminds her of the words the angel Gabriel spoke to her on the day of her Annunciation: "The Holy Spirit will come upon you, and the power of the Most High will overshadow you; therefore the child to be born will be called holy, the Son of God" (Luke 1:35).

Now Mary takes a long, deep breath and pauses. It is as if all creation waits in silence, as if time itself has stopped. Then, in the stillness, comes the sound the world has longed to hear since the Fall, the quiet cry of a newborn child, God-with-Us. The Messiah is born!

Joseph holds the baby in his arms and beholds his sweet and radiant face. Here, cradled in the strong hands of the workman from Nazareth, is the One the world has been waiting for. The almighty God is no longer invisible. Joseph places the baby reverently in Mary's arms. Sitting, she instinctively bows her head over the child, and Joseph kneels by her side. The stillness lingers, as if time itself kneels with them in adoration. Joseph whispers the words of a psalm: "Let your face shine on your servant; save me in your merciful love!" (Psalm 31:16). And Mary, still gazing into the eyes of her baby, replies to her husband in the words of another familiar psalm: "The eyes of the LORD are toward the righteous, and his ears toward their cry" (Psalm 34:15). Outside, in the dark, clear night, a bright star shines. Somewhere far away, wise men continue their long journey toward the star and the infant king whose birth it announces. Meanwhile, a choir of angels gathers above a nearby field, proclaiming joyfully the birth of the Savior to startled shepherds below. But here, in the quiet of the cave, Mary and Joseph remain in silence, knowing nothing yet of the wise men and the angels and shepherds. In their arms they hold the baby, overwhelmed with love and awe as they behold in his tiny features the radiant face of God.

For your prayer

Today will be busy; however, find some time to be alone. Close your eyes, and ask the Holy Spirit to inspire your imagination and guide you as you pray. Imagine the scene above. Be *in* the scene. Be *with* Mary as she gives birth to her son. Imagine that *you* are there as the child is born. Imagine that *you* are with Joseph as he looks upon the face of God and as he kneels in adoration of Jesus resting in his mother's arms. Be there *with* them. Be there in the scene.

What words stood out to you as you prayed?
What did you find stirring in your heart?

_____
_____
_____
_____
_____
_____
_____
_____
_____
_____
_____
_____
_____
_____
_____
_____
_____
_____
_____
_____
_____
_____

PROCLAIM

"For to you is born
this day in the city of
David a Savior, who
is Christ the Lord."

—Luke 2:11

NOTES

[1] *Suscipe* by St. Ignatius of Loyola.

[2] From the album *Endless Years* (United Pursuit Music, 2012).

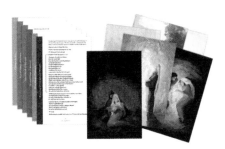

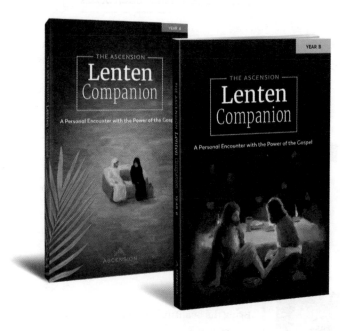